HUMAN BODY
BASICS

There are seven things that you have in common with every single living creature – from trees to tigers, beagles to bacteria. All living things breathe, eat, excrete, grow, move, feel and reproduce. These are the seven life processes.

Cells

Your body is made of tiny building blocks called cells. Each cell is so tiny that it cannot be seen without a microscope. All cells have the same basic parts but the exact structure of each cell depends on its job.

Tissue

Cells of the same type connect together to make a tissue. Different types of tissue then join together to form an organ.

Organs

Organs link together to make systems. Each system takes care of a different life process, such as breathing, eating or moving.

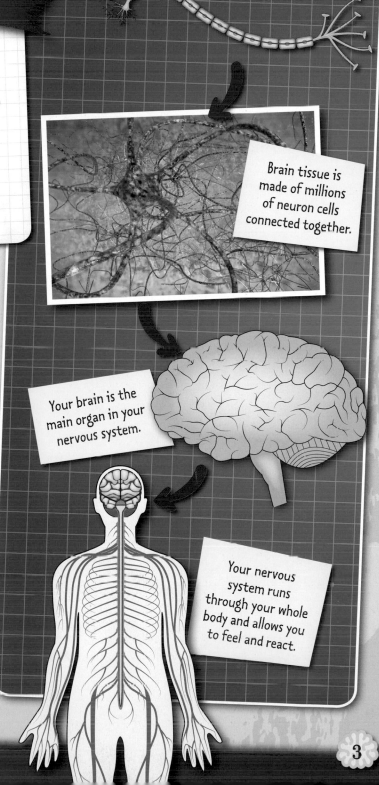

Neurons are specialised cells that make up your brain and nervous system.

Brain tissue is made of millions of neuron cells connected together.

Your brain is the main organ in your nervous system.

Your nervous system runs through your whole body and allows you to feel and react.

3

YOUR MIND-BENDING BRAIN

Your brain makes up just about 2% of your body weight – but it's so energy- and oxygen-hungry that while you're awake, it demands 20% of your body's supplies.

So what does your brain actually do?

The simple answer is, your brain is in charge of everything! Using the nervous system, it sends messages to and fro to make sure you keep breathing, your heart carries on beating, your stomach processes food, it's possible to walk, talk, touch your nose with your fingertip while your eyes are shut, and much more.

Your brain is also a storehouse for memory. It lets you recognise people's faces and understands their expressions to tell you what mood they are in. It remembers language and stores all kinds of information: where you left your phone, or the date of your mum's birthday, for example.

Bits of the brain

The brain is divided into several areas, each of which has its own job to do. One important division is between the right and left sides. Weirdly, the right side of the brain controls the left side of the body, and vice versa.

People with special abilities often have special brains, too. For example, the maths and physics bits of Albert Einstein's brain were a third larger

Albert Einstein

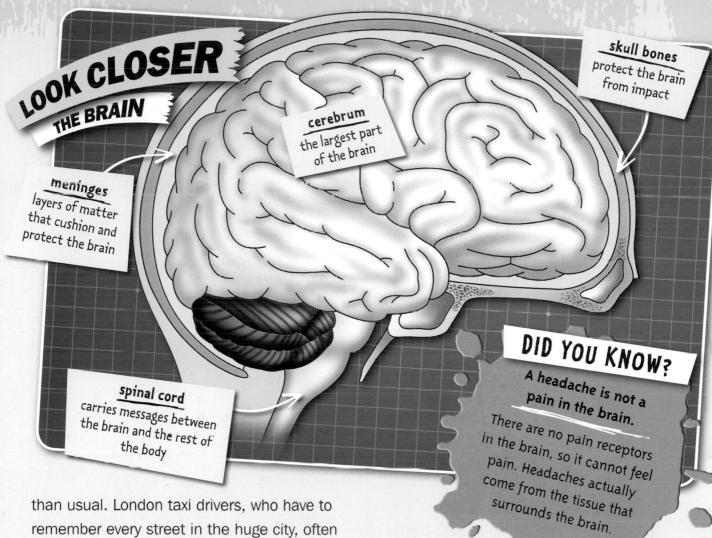

meninges
layers of matter that cushion and protect the brain

cerebrum
the largest part of the brain

skull bones
protect the brain from impact

spinal cord
carries messages between the brain and the rest of the body

DID YOU KNOW?

A headache is not a pain in the brain.

There are no pain receptors in the brain, so it cannot feel pain. Headaches actually come from the tissue that surrounds the brain.

than usual. London taxi drivers, who have to remember every street in the huge city, often have a bigger-than-average hippocampus – the part of the brain associated with memory (see page 17).

Still working while you sleep

While you are asleep, your brain carries on with its background maintenance functions, such as keeping you breathing. But it has a lot of spare capacity – some of which it seems to use for dreams. Everyone has dreams, but not everyone remembers them. Not everyone dreams in colour, either: about 12% of us dream in black-and-white.

DON'T TRY THIS AT HOME!

Brain surgery has a long history – archaeologists have found evidence of crude brain operations being done over 4,000 years ago.

The operation, known as 'trepanning', seems likely to have been an extreme attempt to cure REALLY bad headaches. It was done by drilling a hole in the skull, to try to relieve pressure on the brain. Ouch!

PARTS OF YOUR BRAIN

Your brain is a bit like a football team. It is made up of individual parts working together to do a job. Here are some important parts of your brain and the jobs that they do:

BRILLIANT BODY FACT

Almost all adult brains are a similar size — and there's no proof that a big brain guarantees intelligence.

LOOK CLOSER
PARTS OF THE BRAIN

cerebrum
for thought and conscious action

limbic system
for emotions and memory

brain stem
for basic functions to stay alive, e.g. breathing

cerebellum
for linking together movements

Making plans

Deciding to kick a football at a goal might SOUND simple – but you couldn't make even easy decisions like this without a cerebrum. This is the largest area of the brain, and it's where you do your thinking and planning.

Running and jumping

From walking to skateboarding, surfing or gymnastics… actually, for ANYTHING that involves balance and coordination, you need a cerebellum.

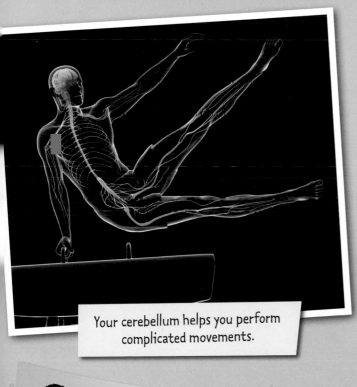

Your cerebellum helps you perform complicated movements.

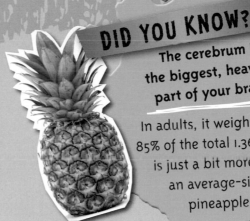

Without thinking

Are you breathing? Is your heart beating? Is your stomach digesting your breakfast? And most importantly, did you have to THINK about doing any of these things?

The answers are yes, yes, yes and no!

The reason is that your brain stem controls all these things (and more) without you having to think about them.

So many emotions

If you're feeling happy, excited or relaxed, you can thank your limbic system. It's also to blame if you start crying or throw a hissy fit, though. This tiny area, buried deep inside the brain, affects emotions. It also helps you form memories.

Feeling happy? That's your limbic system.

GROWING A BRAIN

BRILLIANT BODY FACT

A toddler's brain grows over a million new connections EVERY SECOND!

No baby arrives with a fully developed brain – otherwise the head would be too big for it to be born! Once a baby is born, its brain carries on changing.

A baby's brain begins to develop while it is still in the womb.

Growing synapses – as easy as riding a bike

The key raw material for a brain is a cell called a neuron. As your brain develops, the neurons in various parts of your brain connect, forming links called synapses. These synapses are what allow your brain to work.

To understand the importance of synapses, consider how much better you were at cycling the 100th time you rode a bike than the first time. It's because when you have a new experience, such as riding a bike, your brain develops new synapses. These are like a handbook in your brain – a guide for next time you want to ride a bike.

Once your brain knows how to do it, you do not need to think about how to cycle.

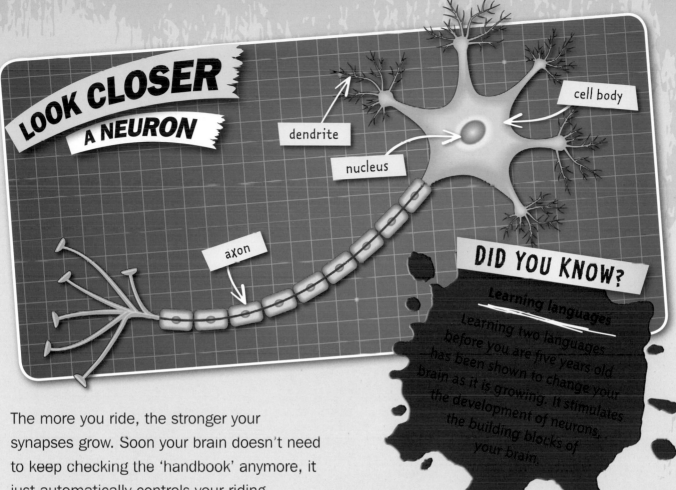

LOOK CLOSER
A NEURON

dendrite

nucleus

cell body

axon

DID YOU KNOW?

Learning languages

Learning two languages before you are five years old has been shown to change your brain as it is growing. It stimulates the development of neurons, the building blocks of your brain.

The more you ride, the stronger your synapses grow. Soon your brain doesn't need to keep checking the 'handbook' anymore, it just automatically controls your riding.

Each new skill you learn, such as learning a new language, stimulates the brain and creates more connections. Learning to juggle can change the brain's structure in about a week!

Too many synapses

By the time you're three years old, you have about 1,000 trillion synapses. Your brain finds it easy to develop new ones until you're about 10 or 11. Then when you're a teenager it starts to prune these down, getting rid of the connections that it doesn't need and making important ones stronger.

DON'T TRY THIS AT HOME!

Back in the Middle Ages, people hadn't yet discovered a reliable anaesthetic.

Before a brain operation, patients drank 'dwale' (lettuce juice, gall from a boar, opium, henbane, hemlock and vinegar) instead. Dwale (say dwaluh) sometimes made patients unconscious — but often it just killed them.

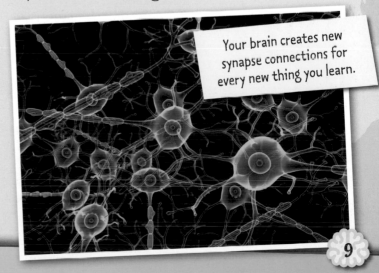

Your brain creates new synapse connections for every new thing you learn.

LEFT SIDE, RIGHT SIDE

You can't help noticing when you look at a brain that it's divided into two sides. The sides constantly communicate with each other, but they do have separate jobs – which is where things get a bit weird.

Separate tasks

The LEFT side of your brain controls the right side of your body and the RIGHT side of your brain controls the left side of your body. No one really knows why.

Not only that, but the left side seems to work mainly on tasks such as language, mathematics and logical thinking. The right side is more interested in music, recognising faces and how you feel about things.

Right-sided, left-sided

One side of your brain tends to be dominant. Researchers think that this is caused by your genes, which are passed on to you from your parents and determine particular characteristics. They have found that genes affect whether you are right- or left-handed.

However, it isn't always that simple. Some people are mixed-handed – they can change hand depending on the task. For example, they may write with their right hand, but use their left hand for batting and throwing in cricket. In rare instances, other individuals are ambidextrous – able to do tasks equally well with either hand.

Helping out

Each area of your cerebrum has a specific job to do. However, if one area is damaged, another can sometimes step into the role. For example, normally your brain needs both right and left sides to process vision – but in Germany, there is a girl who can see despite being born with only one side to her brain.

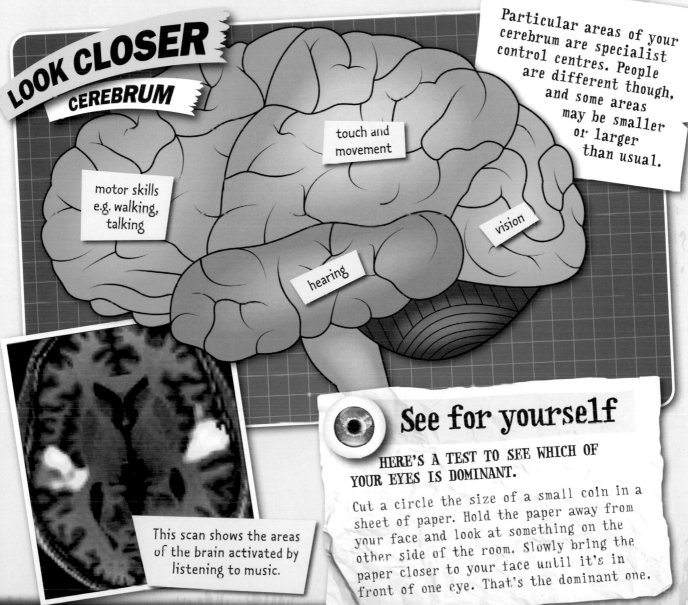

LOOK CLOSER
CEREBRUM

touch and movement

motor skills e.g. walking, talking

vision

hearing

Particular areas of your cerebrum are specialist control centres. People are different though, and some areas may be smaller or larger than usual.

This scan shows the areas of the brain activated by listening to music.

See for yourself

HERE'S A TEST TO SEE WHICH OF YOUR EYES IS DOMINANT.

Cut a circle the size of a small coin in a sheet of paper. Hold the paper away from your face and look at something on the other side of the room. Slowly bring the paper closer to your face until it's in front of one eye. That's the dominant one.

HIGH-SPEED BRAIN WORK

Imagine what would happen if messages to and from your brain ended up in the wrong place. You could mean to kick a ball, but end up poking yourself in the eye!

Delivering instructions

Fortunately, your brain is excellent at making sure messages reach where they're needed. It does this through your nervous system, which is like your body's postal service for instructions. Signals zoom from your brain to the rest of your body (and back again) via the spinal cord – a bundle of nerves running down your backbone.

DID YOU KNOW?

You have about as many neurons in your brain as there are trees in the Amazon rainforest.

When that sentence was written there were about 100 billion trees in the Amazon.

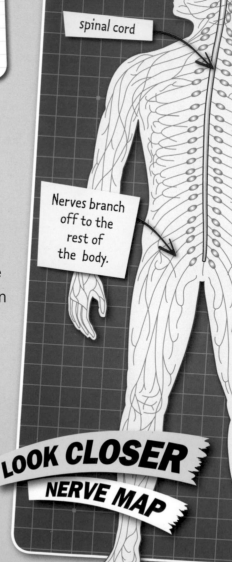

brain

spinal cord

brain stem

Nerves branch off to the rest of the body.

Messages pass from and to the brain.

LOOK CLOSER
NERVE MAP

12

Neural messengers

When a message leaves the brain, it whizzes at high speed down the brain stem and into your nervous system. The 'nerves' that send the messages are neurons, like the cells in your brain. You have three main kinds:

✳ **Sensory neurons** carry messages from the outer parts of your body to the spinal cord.

✳ **Interneurons** connect within the brain and spinal cord.

✳ **Motor neurons** carry messages from the spinal cord to the outer parts of your body.

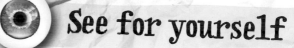

See for yourself

Test the speed of your brain's reactions! Ask a friend to hold a ruler from the highest-numbered end and let it hang down. Put your finger and thumb at zero, but don't touch it. Without warning, your friend lets go: you grab.

Look at the measurement under your thumb, and use the chart below to work out your reaction time:

Distance (cm)	Reaction time (seconds)
5	0.10
10	0.14
15	0.17
20	0.20
25	0.23
30	0.25

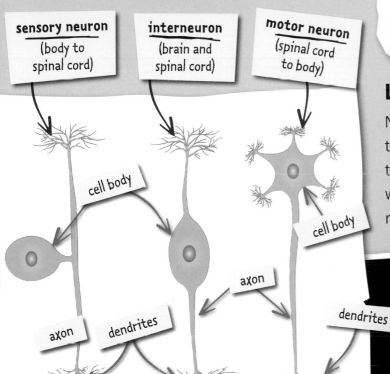

sensory neuron (body to spinal cord)

interneuron (brain and spinal cord)

motor neuron (spinal cord to body)

cell body

cell body

axon

axon

dendrites

dendrites

Long and short

Neurons have arms called axons. Some of the neurons in your fingertip have axons that stretch all the way to your shoulder, while the ones in your brain may be only a millimetre or two long.

In sport, players need to react quickly. The brain sends a message through the nervous system and the body responds!

YOUR BLINKING BRAIN

Mostly, people don't have to think before they blink. Unless they're fluttering their eyes at someone, that is. Their brain just automatically tells their eyelids to close and open again whenever needed.

Brain on autopilot

It's not only blinking: your brain does a whole LOAD of important jobs without you having to think about them. You wouldn't want to have to remember to tell your body to breathe, for example – what would happen when you went to sleep? Fortunately, your brain automatically handles a lot of everyday work for you.

STRANGE BUT TRUE!

Each time we blink, our brains fill in the gap, so that the world doesn't keep going dark. But it doesn't work if you blink deliberately: this makes the blink bigger, so the gap is harder to fill in.

DID YOU KNOW?

Harvard University in the USA has a Brain Bank containing over 7,000 brains.

Scientists use the brains to study the nervous system, and to try to find tests and treatments for diseases that affect the brain.

The amazing brain stem

Although it's a small part of the brain, your brain stem (see page 6) does a lot of the important little jobs that keep you alive (such as making sure your heart beats). Here are just a few of the things your brain manages without being told:

Without a brain stem, no one would get their beauty sleep: one of its jobs is to regulate sleep.

Singing! 10 of the 12 pairs of cranial nerves, which control movement of the face and neck, come from the brain stem.

Breathing would be impossible without a brain stem. It regulates respiration, heartbeat and circulation.

Digestion is also controlled by the brain stem. You stop thinking about food once you have chewed and swallowed, but your body keeps working on it without you thinking about it.

DON'T TRY THIS AT HOME!

The Moscow Brain Institute is home to some famous Russian brains. Among them is the leader of the Russian Revolution, Vladimir Lenin.

Lenin's brain was first investigated in 1926, because officials wanted to discover what had made Lenin such a brilliant leader. Scientists have been studying the brain ever since. It has been cut into 31,000 slices! After all that study, scientists have decided that Lenin's brain was pretty ordinary.

The brain stem connects the brain to the central nervous system: it lets people run around, pose for photos, and much more.

THE BODY'S HARD DRIVE

Information stored in our brains is called 'memory'. Your brain is a bit like a computer's hard drive: it stores images, words, smells and so on.

Are all memories the same?

The answer is no. Experts separate memory into three different categories:

1. **Sensory memory** – information from your senses, usually held for less than a second while the brain decides whether to pay attention to it or not.

2. **Short-term memories** – things you need to remember only for a short time. For instance, to understand this sentence, you have to remember that it's about short-term memory.

3. **Long-term memory** – things you hold on to for a long time, such as your phone number, your friend's name, or how to brush your teeth.

All your experiences can go into making new memories.

What makes a memory?

Memories are made of connections between neurons, called synapses. Each time your brain does something – smelling freshly cut grass, singing a song – the synapses

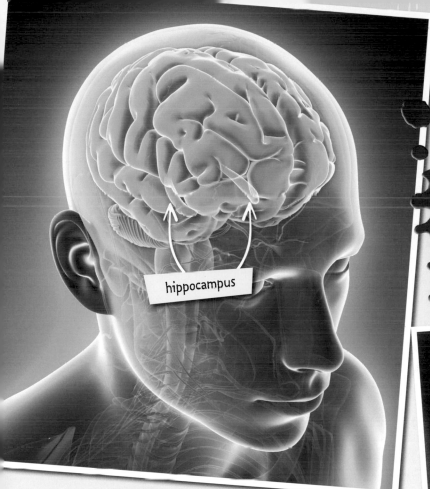

hippocampus

British Prime Minister Winston Churchill (1874–1965) could apparently remember the entire works of Shakespeare.

associated with that action connect more strongly. Memories of places, people or events are often triggered by smells because the parts of your brain dealing with smell, memory and emotion are linked.

The hippocampus

Forming new memories is associated with a part of the brain called the hippocampus. A normal brain has two hippocampuses, one on each side. If one is damaged, the brain can usually shift its memory work completely to the remaining hippocampus. If both are damaged, though, people often have trouble forming new memories, and may even lose old ones.

See for yourself

Test your memory with this simple game. Ask a friend to cut out a photo of a person from a magazine. You have 30 seconds to memorise it, then the photo is put away.

Your friend asks you more and more detailed questions about the picture: you receive a point for each correct answer, but stop when you get two in a row wrong.

SWEET DREAMS

When you're asleep, your brain carries on managing important jobs (such as breathing). But that leaves a lot of spare capacity – some of which it uses for dreaming.

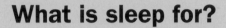

You might not remember your dreams, but you dream every night. We all do!

What is sleep for?

Sleep is a time when your conscious brain turns off, and your body (including your brain) gets a chance to repair itself.

You have two basic sleep modes: Non Rapid Eye Movement (NREM) and Rapid Eye Movement (REM). In NREM sleep, which lasts about 80% of your sleep time, your brain is fairly quiet. During REM sleep, though, it becomes as active as when you're awake. This is when you dream.

You can tell if someone is in REM sleep: their eyes move to and fro underneath their eyelids. At the same time, their muscles are effectively paralysed, so they barely move.

STRANGE BUT TRUE!

The *Guinness Book of Records* no longer has a category for 'Longest without sleep'. Going without sleep is too dangerous for it to be encouraged.

Easy to forget

No one remembers every dream. Most people dream for one to two hours each night, and pack in at least four different dreams. You are most likely to remember dreams if you wake up during them.

What are dreams for?

Surprisingly, experts do not agree on why humans dream – just that everyone DOES dream. Some researchers think dreaming is the brain's way of keeping itself entertained while it doesn't have much else to do. Others think dreams are part of the brain's process of sorting information, deciding what to delete and what to hold on to. Some people believe dreams provide clues to what we are feeling deep down. But no one knows for sure.

Sigmund Freud (1856–1939) thought dreams showed how people were feeling.

DON'T TRY THIS AT HOME!

In 1959, a New York DJ called Peter Tripp went without sleep for 201 hours. After 72 hours he began laughing, then getting upset, for no reason. Next he started hallucinating. Finally he started claiming he wasn't Peter Tripp at all.

Tripp's family said that his personality changed forever: he became moody, depressed and hard to live with.

It's harder to sleep high up a mountain, especially above 4,000m. This is thought to be because of the lack of oxygen in the air.

DID YOU KNOW?

Humans spend about 30% of their lives asleep.

That SOUNDS like a lot — until you realise that cats sleep for about 70% of theirs.

YOUR EMOTIONAL BRAIN

Imagine you're out surfing and a fin rises up beside you. When you think 'AARRRGH! I'M GOING TO BE BITTEN BY A SHARK!' that's your limbic system – sometimes called your 'emotional brain' – swinging into action.

Alarm bells ringing

Your limbic system is a) slightly simple minded and b) very fast acting. So even though you know that *logically* the fin is probably a dolphin, or a non-killer shark, your limbic system quickly sends out a 'be-afraid' message.

Seeing the fin causes neurons to be stimulated and to release 'be afraid' chemical signals called neurotransmitters. These travel across a synapse and are picked up by another neuron. In no time at all, the message passes from neuron to neuron until it reaches the brain.

When the brain receives the signal, it stimulates more neurons to release more

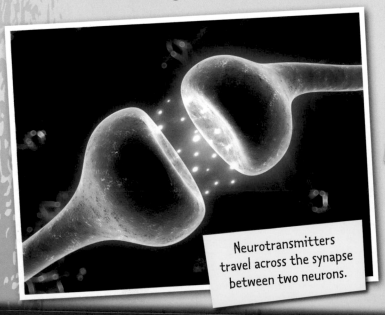

Neurotransmitters travel across the synapse between two neurons.

STRANGE BUT TRUE!

One study has suggested that when people gain power over others, it affects their brains. They become less able to understand what others are feeling.

neurotransmitters. These prepare you to either fight the shark (if it IS a shark), or swim away very quickly. This is the fight-or-flight response.

What causes emotions?

Most experts think that emotions are left over from the early days of humanity. They are preparation for behaving in a particular way. So, for example, when faced with something threatening, our brains generate feelings of either fear or aggression. We're immediately prepared to either fight or run away.

Emotions are not only caused by threats. Happy emotions are the brain's reaction to something good – a nice dinner, scoring a goal, or doing well at school, for example.

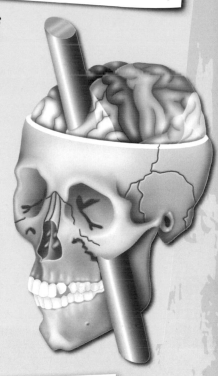

DON'T TRY THIS AT HOME!

Phineas Gage was a railway worker who had a VERY bad day back in 1848.

An explosion at work caused an iron bar to go right through Gage's head, destroying most of the front-left part of his brain. Amazingly, within two months he was able to walk around, and Gage lived for another 12 years.

Happy emotions may be the brain's reaction to doing something well.

YOUR SUPER SENSES

BRILLIANT BODY FACT
You inherit your sense of smell from your parents. If they can smell a smell, you can too!

Your senses swing into action the moment you wake up. From hearing the alarm, to seeing daylight, smelling toast, feeling warm or cold air, tasting orange juice – all these things rely on your senses. But what ARE your senses, and how do they work?

How do senses work?

Your senses rely on receptors – specialised neurons that can detect changes such as brighter light or increased temperature. For example, if you prick your finger this is what happens:

What are senses?

Senses are messages about your environment, sent from your nervous system to your brain. Traditionally humans are said to have five main senses:

✳ **Sight** relies on your eyes.

✳ **Hearing** uses your ears.

✳ **Taste** comes mainly from your tongue.

✳ **Touch** is made up of messages from your skin.

✳ **Smell** relies mainly on your nose.

1. Receptors in your skin sense that it has been damaged.

2. Neurons in your fingertip whiz electrical signals along your arm to the spinal cord.

3. Neurotransmitters (see page 20) pass the message along the spinal cord to the brain.

4. The thalamus decides where the message needs to go: in this case, to the areas of the brain linked with physical sensations, conscious thought and emotions.

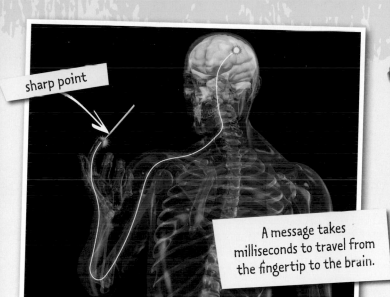

sharp point

A message takes milliseconds to travel from the fingertip to the brain.

LOOK CLOSER
YOUR SKIN

body hair

surface of skin

touch receptors

pain receptors

heat receptors

cold receptors

pressure receptor

Under the skin

One of your most important senses is touch. You receive lots of information whenever you touch something. Below the surface of your skin are lots of specialised receptors. These send your brain messages about your surroundings, such as temperature, pain, pressure and texture (whether something is rough or smooth).

SIGHT AND SOUND

Each of your eyes is as big as a ping-pong ball – but much, much more complicated. Together with your ears, your eyes provide your brain with information about what's going on around you.

From eyeball to brain

An image's journey to the brain begins when light enters your eye. It hits the retina, where millions of light-sensitive cells turn the light into nerve signals. The optic nerve, which carries over a million nerve fibres, sends these signals to the brain. There, your brain attaches labels to what it's seeing: 'rain', 'teacher' or 'killer crocodile', for example.

LOOK CLOSER
YOUR EYE

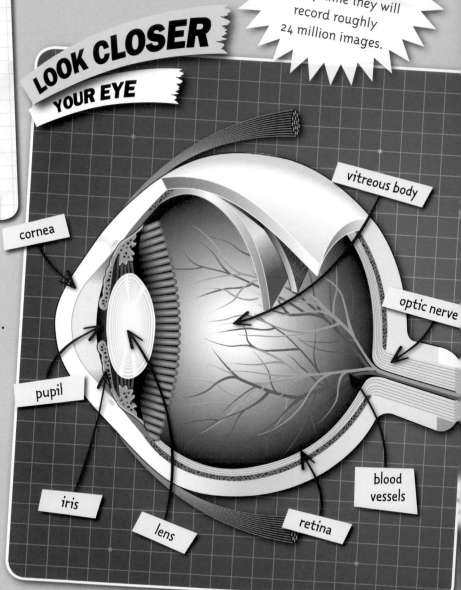

- vitreous body
- cornea
- optic nerve
- pupil
- iris
- lens
- retina
- blood vessels

The blind spot

The retina sends a complete picture of what you see to the brain. But there is a gap where the optic nerve attaches. This is known as the blind spot. Your brain does not register this blind spot, though: it fills in the gap automatically.

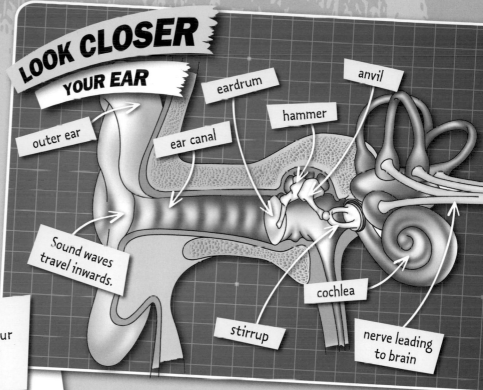

outer ear

ear canal

eardrum

hammer

anvil

Sound waves travel inwards.

stirrup

cochlea

nerve leading to brain

The image your eyes record on your retina is upside down. Fortunately, your brain knows this and automatically turns it the right way up.

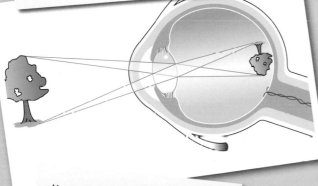

Your senses warn you of danger, from the roar of a tiger to the sight of a car when you're crossing the road.

Your hairy hearing

Your hearing depends on little 'hair cells' in your inner ear. They're not actually hairs: they get their name from little shapes that stick out from the surface of the cell. When sound vibrations enter the ear, hair cells release neurotransmitters (see page 20). Nerves connecting the ear to the brain pick up the neurotransmitter signals and pass them on to the brain for decoding.

See for yourself

THIS EXPERIMENT TESTS WHETHER TWO EARS ARE BETTER THAN ONE.

Mark an X on the floor, then mark lines 2.5m, 5m, 7.5m and 10m away. Blindfold someone standing on the X. Now call their name from various lines keeping your voice at the same volume. Ask them to guess which line you are standing on.

Repeat the exercise, but with the blindfolded person wearing an earplug in one ear. Are they as good at working out the distances?

SMELL
AND TASTE

Most humans have a favourite smell. Usually your favourite reminds you of something good. It might make you feel happy, hopeful, or full of energy. This is because smells and emotions are closely linked. Smell and taste are also closely linked. In fact, most of what you THINK is taste is actually the smell of your food.

Food Safety Alert!

Have you ever spat out a piece of rotten food, which would have given you an upset tummy? If so, you will know that together, smell and taste are an important early-warning system for your body. They help you decide if your food is safe to eat.

Animals have favourite flavours too! Cats apparently like a plant called valerian, lions like mint, and camels like tobacco!

See for yourself

AROUND 80% OF WHAT WE THINK IS TASTE IS ACTUALLY SMELL.

You can test this for yourself by holding your nose next time you eat something. Then taste it again normally. Was the taste stronger or weaker first time?

STRANGE BUT TRUE!

Some people have extra taste buds, plus brains that are super-sensitive to the flavours of food and drink. These people are called supertasters.

Other people have fewer taste buds, and cannot taste as well as normal. And to make matters worse, they don't even get their own special name!

How do we smell?

The air is full of tiny particles called odour molecules. These come from all kinds of sources: cut grass, wood, pencils, cooking food, and many more. Your nose is equipped with special cells called chemoreceptors.

The chemoreceptors pick up molecules when you breathe in or sniff. Each chemoreceptor is specialised, and can only pick up a particular kind of molecule. The chemoreceptor then sends a message to your brain, signalling what kind of molecule has been dctcctcd   in othcr words, what you are smelling.

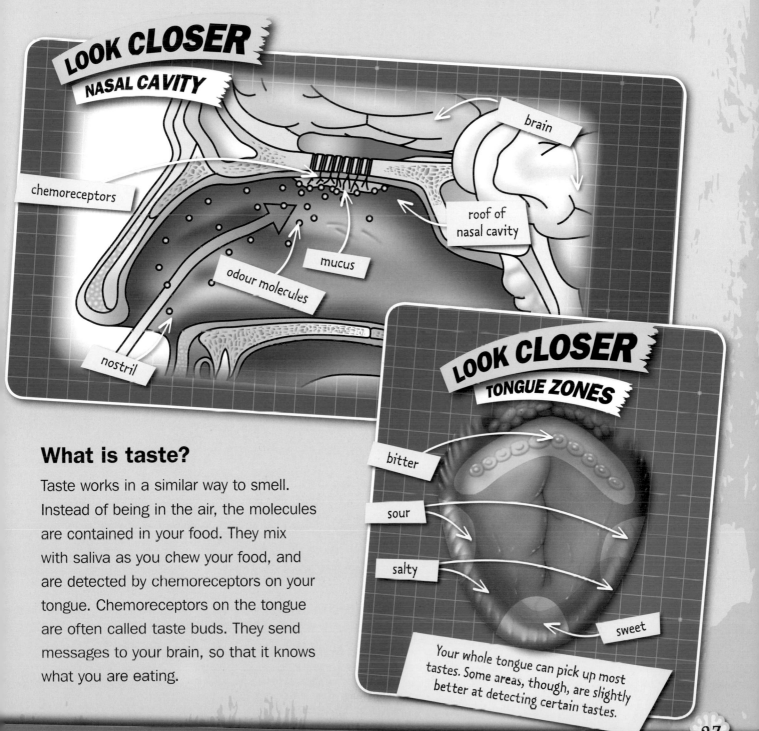

LOOK CLOSER
NASAL CAVITY

chemoreceptors

brain

roof of nasal cavity

mucus

odour molecules

nostril

LOOK CLOSER
TONGUE ZONES

bitter

sour

salty

sweet

Your whole tongue can pick up most tastes. Some areas, though, are slightly better at detecting certain tastes.

What is taste?

Taste works in a similar way to smell. Instead of being in the air, the molecules are contained in your food. They mix with saliva as you chew your food, and are detected by chemoreceptors on your tongue. Chemoreceptors on the tongue are often called taste buds. They send messages to your brain, so that it knows what you are eating.

MAINTENANCE AND SERVICING

You only have one brain, so it pays to keep it working properly. Looking after your brain will mean you do as well as possible at any activity that involves your brain – which is basically ALL activities.

① Keep it working!

Learning new things helps the brain to generate new cells. This is especially true if you learn things that involve both physical and mental activity, such as playing an instrument.

② Eat right!

What you eat affects your brain in lots of ways:

✳ Oily fish such as mackerel and sardines contain essential fatty acids. Eating plenty of these is said to be good for your memory.

✳ A daily sprinkle of pumpkin seeds provides zinc, which your brain needs for memory and conscious thought.

✳ Get fruity! Vitamin C is thought to increase the speed at which your brain can process thoughts. Fruits containing lots of vitamic C include blackcurrants and citrus fruits.

✳ Eating vegetables containing B vitamins has been shown to help older people keep their brains working well.

③ Work out!

This is a big one: exercising makes more blood flow to the brain, which is crucial for keeping it healthy. The extra blood flow increases the number of tiny blood vessels in your brain and helps the growth of synapses.

④ Avoid cigarettes, alcohol and illegal drugs!

Each has been linked to decreased brain function. One study in the USA found that even smoking a single cigarette a day stopped your brain working as well as before. One alcoholic drink a day also affects your brain.

Illegal drugs have a serious negative effect on your brain, too.

⑤ Sleep plenty!

Sleep is crucial for the brain – when their brain functions are tested, people usually do significantly worse when they are tired than after plenty of sleep.

⑥ Wear a helmet!

Banging your head when you're young can damage your brain. Always wear a helmet for activities that risk bumping your head.

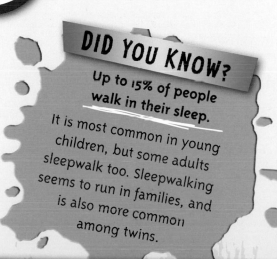

BRAINY WORDS!

ambidextrous able to use either hand equally well

amputee a person who has lost an arm or leg in an accident or operation

axon a long branch of a nerve cell. Messages are sent from the cell body along the axon to other cells.

brain stem part of the brain associated with vital actions such as breathing and digestion

cell the smallest building block from which a living thing is made. Cells are so tiny that they can generally only be seen using a powerful microscope.

cell body the main part of a cell that contains the nucleus

cerebellum part of the brain at the back of the skull, it is associated with movement and balance

cerebrum the largest part of the brain, most often associated with conscious thought and actions

conscious aware of: conscious thoughts and movements are ones you know you are making

dendrite a short branch of a nerve cell that receives messages from other nerve cells via synapses

dominant having power or control over something

evolve to develop slowly, over a long period of time

excrete to get rid of waste products from a living organism

gene a unit of code that passes on characteristics from parents to children

hallucinating seeing things that are not really there

limbic system also called the 'emotional brain', part of the brain associated with emotions and memory

neuron a specialised cell that is able to transmit information through the brain and nervous system

neuroscience the study of the brain and how it works

neurotransmitters chemical signals used by the brain and nervous system to pass messages between neurons

nucleus a cell's control centre

paralysed unable to move

receptors specialised neurons that can detect changes such as brighter light or increased temperature

senses the way you process information about the world around you using your nervous system and your brain

synapse a connection between neurons

thalamus an area deep within the brain, associated with movement, passing sensory messages, and sleep

a neuron

FOOD FOR YOUR BRAIN

Are you hungry for extra information about your brain?
Here are some good places to find out more:

BOOKS TO READ

Future Science Now! *What's next for Medicine?*
Tom Jackson, Wayland 2013

Go Figure: *A Maths Journey through the Human Body,* Anne Rooney, Wayland 2014

The World in Infographics: *Human Body,*
Jon Richards and Ed Simkins, Wayland 2013

MindWebs: *Human Body,*
Anna Claybourne, Wayland 2014

Truth or Busted: *The Fact or Fiction Behind Human Bodies,* Paul Mason, Wayland 2014

WEBSITES

http://kidshealth.org/kid/htbw/brain.html
This website is a really good place to find out all sorts of information about the human body. It has an excellent section on the brain.

www.childrensuniversity.manchester.ac.uk/ interactives/science/brainandsenses/brain/
The Children's University of Manchester, UK, has all sorts of information for kids, presented in the form of labelled illustrations. It includes some easily understood information about the brain, nervous system and senses.

PLACES TO VISIT

In London, the **Science Museum** has regular exhibitions about the human mind, and displays explaining how the body works. The museum is at:

Exhibition Road
South Kensington
London SW7 2DD

The Science Museum also has a really good website, with information about the brain and nervous system, including loads of fascinating facts, here:

www.sciencemuseum.org.uk/whoami/findoutmore/ yourbrain.aspx

The **Natural History Museum** has an amazing 'Human Biology Gallery' where you can get a taste of anything from what a human baby experiences while still inside its mother, through how senses like hearing and smell operate, to the jobs your blood does for you. The museum is at:

The Natural History Museum
Cromwell Road
London
SW7 5BD

The museum also has a good website, the human biology section starts here:

http://www.nhm.ac.uk/visit-us/galleries/blue-zone/ human-biology/

INDEX

WAYLAND

First published in 2015 by Wayland

Copyright © Wayland 2015

Wayland
338 Euston Road
London NW1 3BH

Wayland Australia
Level 17/207
Kent Street
Sydney, NSW 2000

All rights reserved.

Editor: Annabel Stones
Designer: Rocket Design (East Anglia) Ltd
Consultant: John Clancy, Former Senior Lecturer in Applied Human Physiology
Proofreader: Susie Brooks

ISBN 978 0 7502 9237 5
Library eBook ISBN 978 0 7502 9238 2
Dewey categorisation: 612.8-dc23

Printed in China

10 9 8 7 6 5 4 3 2 1

Wayland, part of Hachette Children's Group and published by Hodder and Stoughton Limited
www.hachette.co.uk

Artwork: Ian Thompson: p5 t, p12, p23 c, p25 tr, p25 cl, p27 c; Stefan Chabluk: p3 t, p3 cb, p3 b, p6, p9 t, p11 c, p13 l, p20, p24.

Picture credits: Corbis: p19 bl © Hulton-Deutsch Collection; Getty Images: p4 MPI/Stringer, p14 Bloomberg/Contributor, p17 cr Keystone-France/Contributor, p21 tr BSIP/Contributor, p27 b BSIP/Contributor. Science Photo Library: p7 cl SCIEPRO, p8 t DU CANE MEDICAL IMAGING LTD, p11 bl PR MICHEL ZANCA, ISM. Shutterstock: Cover all, p3 ct, p7 t, p7 b, p8 b, p9 b, p10, p13 b Neale Cousland, p15 r, p15 lb, p16 tl, p16 tr, p16 cl, p16 br, p17 tl, p18 cl, p18 b, p19 cr, p19 br, p21 b, p23 tl, p25 bl, p26 (lion) p26 (mint), p28 b, p28 t p29 t, p29 b. Wikimedia Commons: p5 b CC Some rights reserved/Rama. Graphic elements from Shutterstock.

YOUR BRILLIANT BODY

Marvel at the wonders of the human body with this fact-packed series.

978 0 7502 9388 4

978 0 7502 9246 7

978 0 7502 9240 5

978 0 7502 9237 5

978 0 7502 9249 8

978 0 7502 9243 6

Find out more about the human body with other Wayland titles:

978 0 7502 7868 3

978 0 7502 8158 4

978 0 7502 8241 3

978 0 7502 8280 2